World of Reptiles

Green Iguanas

by Sally Velthaus

Consultants:
The Staff of Reptile Gardens
Rapid City, South Dakota

Capstone press

Mankato, Minnesota

Bridgestone Books are published by Capstone Press,
151 Good Counsel Drive, P.O. Box 669, Mankato, Minnesota 56002.
www.capstonepress.com

Library of Congress Cataloging-in-Publication Data
Velthaus, Sally.
   Green iguanas / By Sally Velthaus.
     p. cm.—(Bridgestone Books. World of reptiles)
     Includes bibliographical references and index.
     ISBN 0-7368-4329-9 (hardcover)
     1. Green iguana—Juvenile literature. I. Title. II. Series.
QL666.L25V45 2006
597.95'42—dc22   2004027946

Summary: A brief introduction to green iguanas, discussing their characteristics, range, habitat, food, offspring, and dangers. Includes a range map, life cycle diagram, and amazing facts.

Editorial Credits
Shari Joffe, editor; Enoch Peterson, set designer; Biner Design, book designer; Patricia Rasch, illustrator;
   Jo Miller, photo researcher; Scott Thoms, photo editor

Photo Credits
Bruce Coleman Inc./Jane Burton, 12; Kim Taylor, cover; Tom Brakefield, 6
Nature Picture Library/Jose B. Ruiz, 16; Pete Oxford, 18; Solvin Zankl, 20
Pete Carmichael, 1
Peter Arnold, Inc./Luiz C. Marigo, 10
Visuals Unlimited/Joe McDonald, 4

Table of Contents

Green Iguanas

A green iguana rests on a tree branch high above a river. Suddenly, a snake slithers near. The iguana leaps into the water below and swims to safety.

Green iguanas are reptiles. All reptiles are **cold-blooded**. They have scales and grow from eggs.

Green iguanas belong to a group of reptiles called lizards. Geckos, skinks, and monitors are also lizards. Green iguanas are related to rock iguanas, desert iguanas, and marine iguanas.

◄ Green iguanas often rest on tree branches.

What Green Iguanas Look Like

Most green iguanas are green, but some are brown, gray, or even bluish. Many green iguanas have dark bands on their tails.

Adult green iguanas are 3 to 6 feet (0.9 to 1.8 meters) long. They have blunt noses and long tails. Green iguanas have four short legs and strong claws. The spines that run down their backs look like a comb.

Males have a flap of skin under their chin called a **dewlap**. The iguana puffs it up with air to scare **predators** or attract a mate.

◀ Green iguanas use their claws for climbing.

Green Iguana Range Map

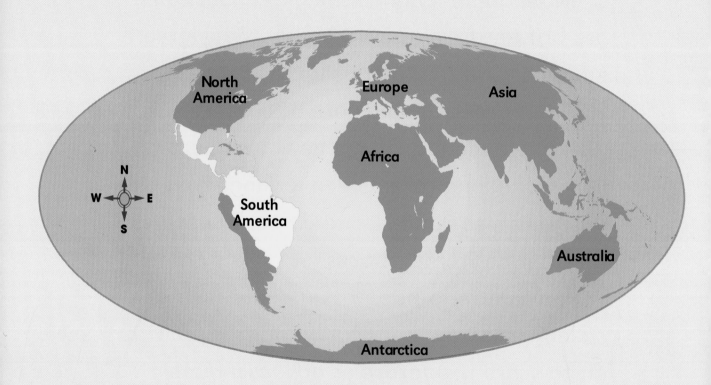

North America

Europe

Asia

Africa

South America

Australia

Antarctica

N
W   E
S

Where Green Iguanas Live

Green Iguanas in the World

Green iguanas live mainly in Mexico and Central America. They are also found in parts of South America. Some green iguanas are found on islands in the Caribbean Sea. Green iguanas were brought to southern Florida. They now live in the wild there.

Green iguanas live in warm, moist areas, especially rain forests. They are usually found near rivers and streams.

Green Iguana Habitats

Green iguanas live in forest **habitats**. They spend most of their time in the tops of trees. They usually choose tree branches that hang over rivers, streams, or ponds. If they sense they are in danger, they drop into the water. A green iguana can fall 50 feet (15 meters) into the water without getting hurt.

Green iguanas also move around on the ground. Like many other reptiles, they sun themselves on rocks or logs to stay warm.

◀ A green iguana suns itself at the top of a tree.

What Green Iguanas Eat

Green iguanas are mainly plant eaters. They like tender leaves, flower buds, fruit, and berries.

Green iguanas sometimes eat meat. They catch small animals such as insects, mice, and birds. They may also eat bird eggs.

Green iguanas do not chew their food. They use their sharp teeth to tear off small pieces. Then they swallow the pieces whole.

◄ A green iguana tears a flower petal from a lily pad.

The Life Cycle of a Green Iguana

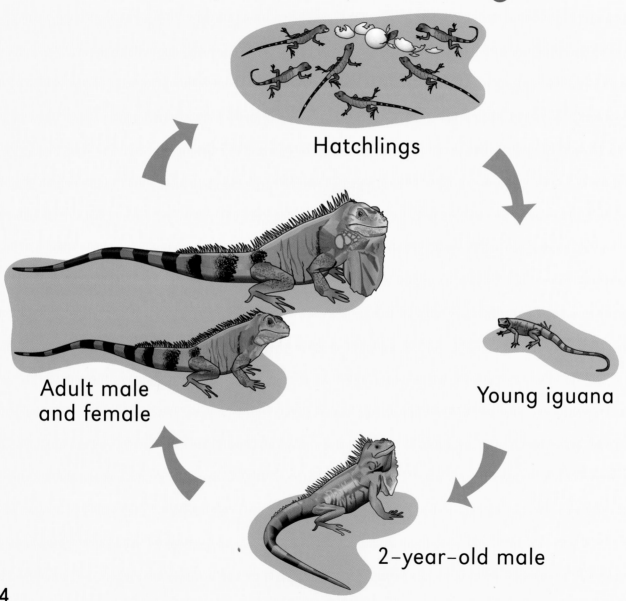

Hatchlings

Young iguana

2-year-old male

Adult male
and female

Producing Young

Male and female green iguanas usually **mate** in the fall. A female chooses a male and then moves to the male's **territory**.

Female iguanas lay 20 to 50 eggs. They hide the eggs in holes, or **burrows**, that they dig in the ground. They also dig fake holes to fool predators that eat iguana eggs.

After females lay eggs, they leave and never return. The eggs hatch about three months later. Hatchlings dig their way out of their burrows to begin their new lives.

Growing Up

Green iguanas take care of themselves as soon as they hatch. Right away they begin searching for food.

Young green iguanas are bright green in color. Their color fades as they get older. As they grow, they **molt**, or shed their skin, about every four to six weeks. White patches appear on the skin when it is ready to shed. Then the skin peels off in pieces.

Green iguanas become adults when they are about 2 years old. They usually live 10 to 12 years.

◂ Young green iguanas grow up completely on their own.

Dangers to Green Iguanas

Green iguanas face many predators. Snakes, large birds, wild dogs, and weasels all hunt iguanas. But humans are the biggest danger to green iguanas. Many people hunt iguanas for food. Others capture them and sell them as pets. People also destroy iguana habitats by clearing forests.

Some people help green iguanas. They raise green iguanas on farms. They sell these iguanas as pets instead of wild iguanas. In some places, people have passed laws to protect green iguanas.

◄ In some countries, such as Guyana, iguanas are sold as meat.

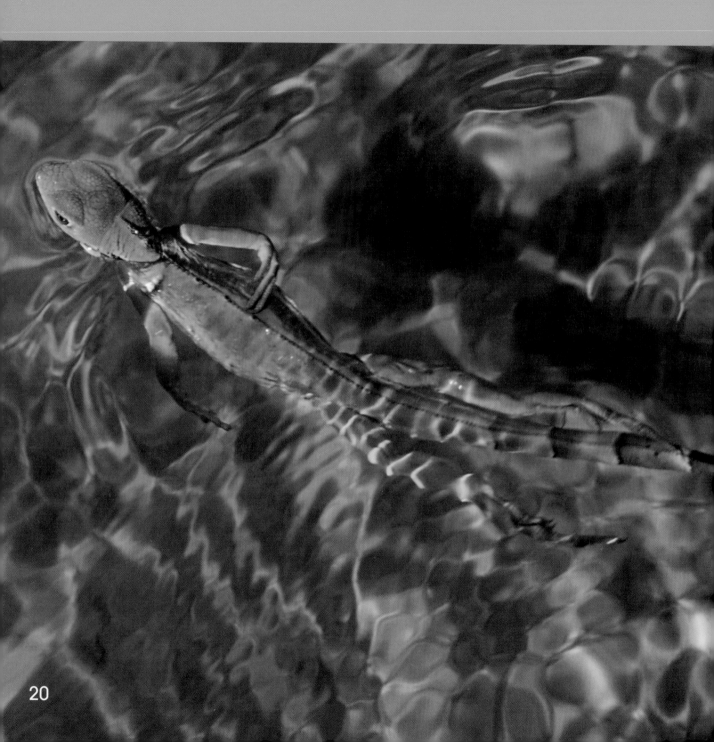

Amazing Facts about Green Iguanas

- Green iguanas are strong swimmers. They can stay underwater for more than 30 minutes at a time.
- Green iguanas often whip their tails at attackers. Their tails are strong enough to break the legs of a small dog.
- Green iguanas are a very common food in some parts of Central America. People there call them "chicken of the tree."

◄ Iguanas swim by using their tails to push themselves through the water.

Glossary

burrow (BUR-oh)—a shallow hole made by a green iguana as a place to lay its eggs

cold-blooded (KOHLD-BLUHD-id)—having a body temperature that is the same as its surroundings; all reptiles are cold-blooded.

dewlap (DOO-lap)—the loose skin that hangs under a lizard's chin or neck

habitat (HAB-uh-tat)—the place and natural conditions where an animal lives

mate (MAYT)—to join together to produce young

molt (MOHLT)—to shed an outer layer of skin

predator (PRED-uh-tur)—an animal that hunts other animals for food

territory (TER-uh-tor-ee)—an area claimed by an animal

Read More

Facklam, Margery. *Lizards: Weird and Wonderful.* New York: Little, Brown, 2003.

Miller, Jake. *The Green Iguana.* Lizard Library. New York: PowerKids Press, 2003.

Internet Sites

FactHound offers a safe, fun way to find Internet sites related to this book. All of the sites on FactHound have been researched by our staff.

Here's how:
1. Visit *www.facthound.com*
2. Type in this special code **0736843299** for age-appropriate sites. Or enter a search word related to this book for a more general search.
3. Click on the **Fetch It** button.

FactHound will fetch the best sites for you!

Index